Entrepreneurial Success Unleashed

Entrepreneurial Success Unleashed

THE BALD AND BONKERS GUIDE TO BUILDING A 6-FIGURE BUSINESS

Sara Larson

Bald and Bonkers Network Academy

Contents

First Printing, 2024

ISBN: 979-8-8691-2080-9
EISBN: 979-8-8691-2081-6

1

Starting Words

In the realm of entrepreneurial aspirations, countless individuals harbor the dream of not only setting up but also steering a flourishing online business, all while embracing the dynamic lifestyle that the internet offers. Despite such dreams, a substantial number of those venturing into the world of online entrepreneurship encounter hurdles. More often than not, the stumbling block lies in the lack of a nuanced approach to laying the foundation for their online enterprise and navigating the intricacies of achieving sustainable success.

The process of establishing a successful online business necessitates more than a mere desire; it calls for a profound understanding of what strategies yield fruitful results and how to circumvent potential pitfalls. Contrary to common perception, embarking on and sustaining a prosperous online business is a more intricate journey than meets the eye. This guide, crafted with a feminine touch, seeks to illuminate the correct approach, offering insights that not only inform but also empower, thereby amplifying your chances of success in the digital realm.

Delving into the pages of this guide, you will discover a wealth of information meticulously curated to equip you with the essential knowledge needed to not only initiate but also navigate the various facets of online entrepreneurship. The content is not only informative but also designed to be easily absorbed, ensuring an engaging and accessible read. We extend an invitation for you to immerse yourself fully in this comprehensive guide, encouraging you to traverse its entirety before embarking on the exciting journey of implementing the invaluable tips and advice it presents.

Furthermore, gain a profound understanding of the strategies embraced by accomplished female entrepreneurs that have paved the way for their success. Learn from their experiences, and in doing so, sidestep the common pitfalls that tend to ensnare new online business owners. This guide serves as a compass, guiding you through the nuanced landscape of online entrepreneurship with a feminine perspective, empowering you to not only dream but to realize those dreams successfully in the competitive digital landscape.

2

Embracing the Online Business Odyssey

Setting Sail into the Digital Entrepreneurial Frontier

In the vast landscape of entrepreneurial pursuits, the decision to embark on the journey of online business is one that opens doors to unprecedented opportunities. The allure of building a business in the digital realm, as opposed to the traditional brick-and-mortar avenues, is fueled by a myriad of enticing reasons that weave a tapestry of advantages unique to the online sphere.

- **Cost-Effectiveness**: Launching an online business is notably more cost-effective than its physical counterpart. The absence of significant upfront costs allows for a more accessible entry into the entrepreneurial world.

- **Staffing Freedom**: Unlike the conventional model of brick-and-mortar establishments, online ventures grant entrepreneurs the liberty to operate without an immediate need for a hired workforce. This not only reduces initial financial burdens but also offers unparalleled flexibility.

- **Spatial Independence**: The absence of a physical office or commercial premises liberates entrepreneurs from the constraints of a fixed location. This flexibility fosters a dynamic business model adaptable to changing circumstances.

- **Instant Commencement**: Online entrepreneurship allows for immediate initiation. The agility of starting a business promptly is a distinctive advantage in the rapidly evolving digital landscape.

- **Minimal Requirements**: All that stands between an aspiring entrepreneur and their online business is a computer or mobile device and a reliable internet connection. This minimalistic requirement makes entrepreneurship more accessible to a diverse range of individuals.

- **Workplace Flexibility**: The ability to operate an online business from any location and set one's working hours is a hallmark of the digital age. This flexibility accommodates various lifestyles and preferences.

- **Adaptation to Digital Commerce**: The prevalence of online transactions in contemporary society positions online businesses strategically. Capitalizing on the trend of digital commerce provides a competitive edge in the marketplace.

- **No Technical Expertise Required**: Contrary to common misconceptions, navigating the online business world doesn't demand extensive technical skills. The democratization of technology has made online entrepreneurship accessible to individuals with diverse backgrounds.

- **Outsourcing Opportunities**: Delegating tasks to freelancers emerges as a viable strategy, allowing entrepreneurs to focus on core business aspects while leveraging specialized skills as needed.

Contrastingly, envisioning the establishment of a physical shop in a bustling mall conjures images of substantial financial investments in inventory, commercial rent, and personnel. Moreover, the amplification of marketing efforts is essential to attract potential customers and make the venture viable.

Part-Time Pursuits Leading to Full-Time Success

The transition into online entrepreneurship need not be an all-encompassing commitment from the outset. Many successful entrepreneurs managing six-figure online enterprises initiated their ventures from the comfort of their homes. The absence of a formal office and the flexibility to determine one's working hours exemplify the unique advantages of online business.

For those currently reliant on a job to meet financial obligations, maintaining that stability while gradually developing the online business during spare time is a prudent strategy. Open communication with family members is crucial to gain their understanding and support during this transitional phase.

The challenge of juggling a full-time job with the commitment required for an online business demands considerable dedication and motivation. A later section will delve into goal-setting strategies and effective ways to stay motivated, essential elements for sustained success.

Acknowledging Risks and Committing to Success

Unfortunately, a significant number of individuals initiating online businesses face the risk of failure. While specific statistics on the reasons are unavailable, a common cause likely stems from a lack of seriousness in approaching the online business endeavor.

The low financial barrier to entry often results in individuals giving up when immediate results are not forthcoming. The initial effort to set up the business may be exerted, but interest wanes quickly. This guide aims to prevent such outcomes by encouraging a steadfast commitment to the online business journey.

No Room for Instant Miracles

The online business realm is rife with hype, promising instant fortunes with minimal effort. However, the reality is that building a six-figure online business requires time and sustained effort. Beware of products that rely on temporary loopholes, as these can lead to an abrupt cessation of income.

Dispelling the notion of instant success, this guide emphasizes the importance of building a sustainable online business. Claims of generating buyer traffic in less than a minute or transforming a computer into an ATM are debunked. Caution is advised against falling for extravagant promises.

Navigating the Online Business Landscape

In the past, online scams led to financial losses

for many individuals. Although such scams have diminished over the years, caution remains essential. Thoroughly vet any products or services before purchasing for online business endeavors.

Initiating Your Online Presence: Domain Name and Hosting

For those serious about online business, owning a domain name is crucial. While free services like Blogger.com, WordPress.com, and Weebly.com exist, investing in a domain name and web hosting is recommended for a more professional image.

Opting for a .com domain from Namecheap.com (priced under $10 a year) and securing web hosting (starting from $5 a month) ensures a solid online presence. The importance of selecting a web host offering various features will be explored in the section on setting up your website.

In conclusion, starting with a modest investment of a $10-a-year domain name and $5–$15-a-month web hosting allows for a strong beginning in the online business landscape. The next chapter will delve into the diverse online business models available for your consideration, providing a comprehensive guide for aspiring online entrepreneurs. As we navigate this digital odyssey together, the horizon of possibilities awaits those with the courage to embrace the entrepreneurial journey in the ever-evolving digital frontier.

3

Embarking on the Quest for the Perfect Online Business Model

As the canvas of your entrepreneurial journey unfolds, the pivotal decision of selecting the right business model becomes the linchpin for success. Each model, meticulously covered in this section, not only harbors the potential for a thriving 6-figure business but also brings with it a unique set of opportunities and challenges. The crux of your journey lies in the careful curation of the model that seamlessly aligns with your preferences and comfort level.

The Art of Navigating Niches

In the vast expanse of online business possibilities, the choice of niche plays a crucial role in shaping the trajectory of your venture. Whether you boast expertise in a particular niche or harbor the willingness to immerse yourself in learning, the selection process necessitates a nuanced consideration of two fundamental factors:

1. **Demand:** Is there a substantive demand for the chosen niche?
2. **Profitability:** Does the niche offer lucrative money-making opportunities?

Opting for an evergreen niche ensures a continuous influx of demand throughout the year, creating a robust foundation for sustainable growth. While our top 3 evergreen niches—Wealth Creation, Health and Fitness, and Personal Development—stand as tried-and-tested options, the dynamic nature of the online landscape encourages exploration of other expansive niches.

Unveiling the Tapestry of Online Business Models

Affiliate Marketing: The realm of affiliate marketing unfolds as an accessible avenue for aspiring online entrepreneurs. Its concept is elegantly simple —vendors pay commissions for bringing in new customers. The role of an affiliate marketer involves the promotion of products and services without the burden of product delivery or customer service. The allure lies not only in its simplicity but also in the flexibility to endorse both physical and digital products.

CPA Marketing: Diverging from the conventional affiliate model, CPA (Cost Per Action) marketing liberates entrepreneurs from the need to secure sales for commission. Instead, commissions are earned through specific actions, such as providing an email address or phone number. While some CPA offers may yield lower commissions, the inherent advantage lies in higher conversion rates compared to traditional affiliate marketing.

Creating Your Own Product or Service: Crafting bespoke products and services tailored to the specific needs of your niche stands as a formidable strategy for constructing a 6-figure online business. While it demands an investment of time, effort, and often finances, the payoff comes in the form of customer ownership—a distinct advantage over the affiliate marketing model.

Ecommerce: Venturing into the realm of e-commerce offers entrepreneurs the prospect of selling physical products through their online store. The process has become more accessible with platforms like Shopify and WordPress offering user-friendly solutions. Success in e-commerce hinges on the strategic selection of the right niche, products, and effective marketing strategies.

Dropshipping: Dropshipping emerges as a captivating model by eliminating the necessity of maintaining inventory. Dropshipping websites handle product ranges and delivery, leaving entrepreneurs to focus on the art of marketing. However, the potentially lower commission levels may necessitate higher sales volumes to achieve significant income.

Drop-servicing: In the landscape of service

arbitrage, drop-servicing emerges as a relatively new but promising concept. The core principle involves offering services to customers at a premium while outsourcing to freelancers at a lower cost. Success in drop-servicing relies on meticulous service selection and establishing relationships with reliable freelancers.

Freelance Services: If you wield a skill in demand, offering freelance services through platforms like Upwork, Freelancer, Fiverr, and PeoplePerHour becomes a viable pathway to a 6-figure online business. These platforms serve as virtual marketplaces where entrepreneurs can showcase their skills, bid for projects, or offer predefined gigs.

Amazon FBA: Leveraging the power of Amazon's Fulfilled by Amazon (FBA) service opens doors to selling physical products on one of the world's largest online marketplaces. While it demands an upfront investment in product acquisition, successful products can yield substantial returns. However, navigating Amazon's stringent rules and regulations is imperative for a successful FBA venture.

Self Publishing: For the wordsmiths among us, the world of self-publishing beckons. Platforms like Amazon KDP, Ingram Spark, or the Bald and Bonkers Network LLC Author Membership offer a canvas for writers to share fiction or nonfiction works without the need for external approval. Success in self-publishing hinges on strategic marketing to attract a broad audience and can potentially result in a 6-figure income.

As we conclude this deep dive into the spectrum of online business models, the journey ahead beckons. The next chapter will unfold the practical steps of setting up your 6-figure online business, guiding you through the intricacies of this digital odyssey. The possibilities are boundless for those ready to embrace the chosen path wholeheartedly and navigate the nuanced landscapes of the digital realm.

4

Unveiling the Tapestry: Crafting Your 6-Figure Online Odyssey

Creating a Digital Masterpiece: The Symphony of Website Creation

Embarking on the pursuit of a 6-figure online empire requires the crafting of a digital masterpiece — a website that not only serves as a storefront but narrates the compelling story of your brand. Even within the realm of Amazon FBA, where giants dominate, having a personal website elevates your venture, adding an extra layer of credibility and commitment to your audience.

Selecting Your Digital Identity: The Ballet of Domain Name

As you prepare for your digital performance, the careful selection of a domain name becomes a nuanced ballet. The .com extension, akin to a prima ballerina, stands as the preferred lead, but the stage is adorned with alternatives like .net and .org, each pirouetting with its unique charm. An ensemble of newer extensions — .co, .club, .news, .review, and more — awaits its moment in the spotlight.

Should your aspirations be rooted in a specific locale, a country-specific extension, such as .co.uk or .com.au, adds a touch of local flair. For a global performance, the classic trio of .com, .net, or .org remains a timeless choice. These domains are revered as global virtuosos, commanding superior resonance, especially in the intricate art of search engine ranking.

Whether you opt for a name that whispers meaning or a branded symphony, the domain choice orchestrates your brand's melodic journey. While a name like clothesforall.com directs visitors with clarity, a brand like asos.com weaves its recognition through the fabric of marketing endeavors.

Securing a .com domain won't deplete your coffers; a mere annual investment of less than $10 from esteemed registrars like Namecheap or GoDaddy grants you entry to the digital realm. Hyphens are adversaries in this ballet, and .info domains, though thrifty, often waltz away with an air of cheapness. A yearly investment in a stellar domain is an overture to lasting impressions.

Hosting: Where Your Digital Symphony Resides

For your website to pirouette gracefully across the digital stage, a symphony of web hosting is required. Amidst the myriad hosting providers, each offering varied plans and pricing, the overture usually begins with shared hosting. As the crescendo of your traffic grows, the option to ascend to VPS hosting or even command your private server awaits.

In the realm of hosting, speed is the heartbeat. Servers adorned with the latest SSD (solid-state drive) attire not only elevate performance but also dance harmoniously with the impatience of online visitors. Seek hosting partners whose servers are the agile dancers in this digital ballet, ensuring a swift and seamless experience.

When auditioning potential hosts, scan for the following notes in their shared hosting plans:

- Unlimited disk space
- Unlimited bandwidth
- Swift SSD servers
- Complimentary SSL certificates
- Effortless one-click WordPress install
- cPanel access for a choreography of management
- Free malware monitoring and removal to guard against unseen adversaries

The question of domains arises. If your aspirations involve nurturing more than one digital offspring, a shared hosting plan supporting multiple domain names proves an economical choice. The enchanting harmony of resources and affordability often graces such plans.

The essence of one-click WordPress installation is the choreography that transforms your digital canvas. WordPress, a maestro in content management, allows even those without technical prowess to compose symphonies of pages and posts. A deft selection of themes and plugins adds layers of richness to your ballet, creating a tapestry of visual delight and functionality.

Designing Your Emblem: The Ballet of Logos

For the digital prima donna aspiring to a 6-figure crescendo, the visual identity is paramount. A professional logo is the pirouette that elevates your website's aesthetic. Venture not into the perilous choreography of self-designed logos if the steps elude your design sensibilities. Glide gracefully to Fiverr.com, where skilled logo artisans await to craft a visual masterpiece for a mere $25.

Collecting Digital Bouquets: The World of Payment Processors

In the grand theater of online commerce, the collection of bouquets (or payments) demands an orchestration worthy of applause. Whether you're peddling your creations or orchestrating an e-commerce symphony, a reliable payment processor is your trusty conductor.

PayPal, the virtuoso of the digital orchestra, stands tall with millions of patrons and reasonable transaction fees. Yet, the caveat is its uneven global presence. The international stage welcomes alternatives like 2Checkout.com, encompassing a broader array of countries, and Stripe, a rising star in the payments galaxy. The wise conductor conducts research to ensure seamless withdrawals and a harmonious duet with the chosen payment processor.

Capturing the Rhythms of Connection: The Ballet of Email Autoresponders

As your digital ballet unfolds, capturing the rhythms of connection through email marketing becomes a graceful pas de deux. An email autoresponder serves as the ethereal partner in this dance, capturing email addresses and orchestrating seamless communication.

In this realm, Aweber.com and GetResponse.com are the esteemed choreographers, offering sequences of automated emails and a broadcast facility for impromptu notes. Mailchimp, Sendlane, Constant Contact, and others add their unique flair to the ballet.

The ballet continues with an exploration of goal-setting in the next chapter — a roadmap to guide your graceful strides in the vast expanse of the digital stage. Envision the standing ovations; they're not just a dream but a prelude to the symphony you're about to compose.

5

∿

Blossoming Ambitions: Nurturing Your Online Business with Purpose

In the enchanting garden of digital dreams, this chapter unfolds as a mesmerizing sonnet, an ode to those who dare to dance with destiny. A refrain echoes through the petals – to skip this chapter is to miss the crescendo of guidance, a tapestry woven with the threads of success. While the directive may seem resolute, within the realm of femininity, it beckons as an invitation to a dance where goals and aspirations pirouette gracefully.

The Labyrinth of Online Business

Imagine this online journey as a secret garden awaiting tender care. Many, lured by the promise of a flourishing empire, falter in the labyrinth of ambition. Often, the silent saboteur is the absence of a plan or purposeful goals, casting a shadow over the dreams that could have blossomed. The digital realm, akin to a secret garden, beckons with allure and challenge—a canvas where dreams are painted with cautious optimism, petals waiting to unfurl.

The Dance of Persistence

In the ballet of digital entrepreneurship, persistence is the gentle waltz that intertwines with each step. The melody of success is not merely about replicating others' choreography; it is about sculpting your own rhythm. Resilience becomes the nurturing touch, complemented by the delicate art of setting goals and crafting a plan—a canvas where your aspirations take vibrant form.

Choreographing Dreams: Setting Goals with Grace

As the architect of your online destiny, envision

the financial ballet you wish to grace the stage in the inaugural year. In the world of blossoming digital blooms, most novice entrepreneurs overlook this delicate choreography. Yet, dear reader, the heartbeat of your online venture lies in the tender aspirations you dare to set forth.

In the delicate cadence of this guide, serenading the creation of a 6-figure online masterpiece, let your first-year goal pirouette gracefully, whispering a sumptuous $100,000. Can such a spectacle be realized? Indeed, many have pirouetted beyond this threshold, guided not just by numbers but by a sacred ensemble of goals, plans, and the resonating chords of a WHY statement.

If the grandeur of six figures feels like a majestic crescendo, let the ballet sway gracefully to a $50,000 overture. Decide upon this figure, let it be the prima ballerina of your dreams. Engage in the grace of the SMART goal-setting process, where each movement holds significance:

- **Specific**: A lyrical specificity—$50,000 in 12 months, casting a focused spotlight.

- **Measurable**: A dance where each monthly earning is a measured pirouette, marking progress.
- **Achievable**: In this ballet of dreams, acknowledge the journey—no overnight leaps to thousands.
- **Realistic**: Is it within the realm of reality to dance through a $50,000 yearly pas de deux? Indeed, it is!
- **Timed**: A dance where the choreography spans 12 months, every movement aligned to the rhythm of achievement.

Inscribe your goal, let the ink be the ethereal brush that paints your aspirations. Why pen to paper? The secrets lie within the unspoken poetry that unfurls when dreams are penned.

Embodied Dreams: The Euphoria of Achievement

How does your goal weave through the fabric of your being? In this enchanting ballet of dreams, visualize the melody of money cascading into your account. Feel the pride swell within, for you are the orchestrator of an online creation born from the sacred void. Imbue your goal with the hues of emotion, describe the ballet of emotions that will ensue upon its achievement. Carry this sacred parchment with you, a talisman against the winds of uncertainty.

The Heartbeat Beneath: Unveiling the WHY Statement

A goal, even one splendidly crafted, needs a heartbeat—a WHY statement that pulses with purpose. In this dance of digital dreams, delve beyond the surface of monetary aspirations. Who is the silent protagonist in your ballet? Is it for a cherished dream, a profound relationship, or an impact that transcends the mundane pursuit of wealth?

Compose a WHY statement, a poetic narrative that harmonizes with the symphony of your soul. Who are you dancing for? Write these reasons down, carry them as the delicate corsage that adorns your dance attire, a reminder of the profound purpose propelling your dance.

Morning Ballet: A Ritual of Aspiration

As dawn illuminates the stage of a new day, immerse yourself in the rituals that infuse your journey with grace. Read your written goal and WHY statement, let the words be the overture to the day's ballet. In moments of stagnation, when motivation wavers, revisit these affirmations to reignite the passion within. The path to a flourishing online ballet is adorned with challenges; a morning ritual infused with aspirations becomes the tiara that crowns your resilience.

The forthcoming chapters shall unfurl the ballet of strategies, each step a pirouette towards the crescendo of success. As you inscribe your goals and dance with your WHY, envision not just a digital journey but a ballet of dreams, emotions, and the unwavering spirit of a digital ballerina. Let the dance continue, the crescendo building, and the garden of online dreams flourishing in the tender care of your aspirations.

6

Enchanting Traffic Ballet: A Symphony of Digital Elegance

Step into the ethereal realm of traffic generation, where the dance of visitors swirls around your online business like graceful ballerinas on a mesmerizing stage. Traffic, the lifeblood of digital success, holds the power to transform a modest online venture into a thriving spectacle. In this extended exploration, we shall delve into the delicate art of traffic generation, unraveling the enchanting threads that weave success in the online sphere.

The Dance of Visitors: A Prelude to Success

In the ballet of online commerce, traffic takes center stage. Imagine your online business as a grand theater, and each visitor as a cherished attendee eager to witness the spectacle you offer. Even if your offerings are as delicate as a fragile petal, the flood of visitors can turn it into a flourishing bouquet. Conversely, the most exquisite offering in the world may wither in obscurity without the spotlight of attentive eyes.

Traffic Unveiled: A Short but Pivotal Performance

This chapter, though brief, carries the weight of importance. Often, the elegy of online dreams is sung by those who failed to summon a captivating audience to their digital stage. In the intricate ballet of online endeavors, the equation is simple: No traffic equals no online business.

The enchanting secret lies in the myriad ways traffic can be summoned to grace your digital realm. Fear not, for the avenues are diverse, ranging from the graceful pirouettes of free traffic methods to the swift glides of paid methods. While the former demands patience and time, the latter offers a swifter rhythm, allowing you to fine-tune your performance based on paid audience reactions.

Broad Traffic: The Grand Assembly with Limited Allure

Picture a bustling ballroom where vendors promise tens of thousands of attendees for a nominal fee. This is the allure of broad traffic, a gathering where the audience is a diverse spectrum. While tempting, this approach often falls short, as a vast majority may merely glance and move on. Broad traffic, akin to casting a wide net, rarely brings forth a substantial harvest.

Targeted Traffic: A Ballet of Relevance and Engagement

Now, envision a more intimate gathering—visitors with a genuine interest in the tales your online performance narrates. Suppose you guide individuals on the art of making money online; the allure lies in seeking an audience inherently intrigued by this narrative. This is the essence of targeted traffic, where the resonance between your offerings and audience interests blooms into conversion.

As the conductor of this online symphony, dedicate a significant portion of your time—80%, to be precise—to the graceful art of targeted traffic generation. The logic is as simple as it is profound: The more visitors gracing your digital stage, the grander the success of your online performance.

Analogies in Bloom: From Mall Shops to Digital Boutiques

Let's draw a parallel. Picture a quaint shop in a bustling mall. If no visitors grace its threshold, no transactions unfold. The same holds true for your online business. Without the gentle footsteps of digital visitors, the melodies of financial success remain unheard. Traffic generation is not merely a facet; it is the pivotal orchestrator of prosperity, especially when aspiring for the illustrious realm of 6-figure achievements.

The Symphony Extends: A Deeper Dive into Traffic Elegance

Just as a symphony unfolds across multiple movements, so does the exploration of traffic generation deserve an extended composition. Let's navigate through the nuances of both free and paid traffic methods, unraveling the intricate steps that contribute to the graceful dance of visitors around your digital stage.

Free Traffic Methods: The Delicate Waltz of Patience

Embarking on the journey of free traffic is akin to a slow waltz, requiring patience and precision. Engage in the art of content creation—blog posts, articles, and captivating visuals that beckon visitors to linger. Social media platforms, the ballrooms of the digital age, offer spaces to share your narrative and allure a curious audience. The slower tempo may test your patience, but the resonance it creates is worth the meticulous dance.

Paid Traffic Methods: The Swift Ballet of Precision

In the realm of paid traffic, envision a swift

ballet—a choreography of precision and agility. Advertising platforms, like stages awaiting your performance, beckon with the promise of immediate attention. Craft compelling ad campaigns, each step measured, ensuring that every penny spent contributes to the grandeur of your online spectacle. It's a dynamic dance, demanding constant refinement as you gauge the audience's reactions and adjust your movements accordingly.

The Flourish of Blossoms: Leveraging SEO as a Floral Tapestry

Picture your online presence as a garden, with SEO (Search Engine Optimization) as the floral tapestry that enhances its beauty. Delve into the art of optimizing your content, allowing the search engines to discover and showcase your digital blooms. Each keyword, a delicate petal, contributes to the overall vibrancy, attracting the right bees—your targeted audience—to partake in the nectar of your offerings.

Content Creation: The Artistry of Digital Storytelling

Extend your gaze to the realm of content creation—a realm where words and visuals intertwine to create a captivating narrative. In the grand tapestry of online success, your content serves as the brushstroke that paints vivid landscapes for your audience. From engaging blog posts to visually arresting images, each piece of content is a brush dipped in the hues of your brand story.

Craft content that resonates with the desires and aspirations of your audience. Whether it's a heartfelt blog post, an insightful video, or an eye-catching infographic, let your content be the beacon that guides digital wanderers to your online sanctuary. This is not merely information; it's an invitation to step into the world you've created.

Social Media Alchemy: Transforming Platforms into Digital Havens

As you traverse the enchanting landscape of digital success, the role of social media emerges as a potent spell. Social platforms are not mere stages;

they are alchemical cauldrons where your brand essence undergoes transformative processes. From Facebook's communal hearth to Instagram's visual enchantments, each platform offers a unique potion to infuse life into your online presence.

Engage with your audience authentically. Respond to comments, share behind-the-scenes glimpses, and let your brand resonate with the collective heartbeat of your followers. Social media is not just a megaphone for your brand; it's a conversation, a dance of reciprocity where your audience becomes an integral part of the narrative you're crafting.

Video Sorcery: Unleashing the Power of Visual Storytelling

Amidst the digital symphony, the crescendo of video storytelling emerges as a compelling aria. Videos, the visual poetry of the online world, possess the ability to captivate, resonate, and linger in the minds of your audience. From immersive product showcases to heartfelt behind-the-scenes narratives, let your videos be the cinematic masterpiece that elevates your brand.

Consider exploring platforms like YouTube, TikTok, or Instagram Reels to showcase the dynamic facets of your brand. Embrace the magic of storytelling through moving images, and watch as your online presence transforms into a visual tapestry that leaves a lasting imprint.

Influencer Alchemy: Harnessing the Charms of Digital Ambassadors

Within the enchanting corridors of digital success, influencers stand as alchemists, capable of transmuting brand recognition into a widespread phenomenon. Collaborate with influencers whose aura aligns with your brand ethos. These digital sorcerers possess the power to amplify your brand message, casting spells of authenticity and credibility.

The key lies not in the size of the influencer's following but in the resonance of their connection with the audience. Choose influencers whose magic mirrors the essence of your brand, creating an authentic partnership that transcends mere promotion. In the realm of influencer alchemy, it's not just about exposure; it's about weaving genuine connections that endure.

Email Enchantment: Crafting Spells of Connection

As we navigate the labyrinth of digital success, the ancient art of email enchantment reveals itself as a timeless spell. Email marketing, a conduit of direct communication, allows you to weave intricate spells of connection with your audience. Craft newsletters that transcend mere updates; let them be epistles that resonate with the hearts of your subscribers.

Segment your email lists to tailor spells for different segments of your audience. From exclusive offers to heartfelt narratives, each email is a chapter in the ongoing saga of your brand. As the inbox becomes a sacred space, treat each communication as a cherished scroll, carrying the essence of your brand's magic.

Paid Prominence: Unveiling the Elegance of Digital Advertising

As the symphony of online success continues, the allure of paid prominence becomes an enchanting movement. Digital advertising, a choreography of precision, allows your brand to take center stage amidst the vast digital auditorium. Platforms like Google Ads, Facebook Ads, or Instagram Ads offer canvases for your brand to unfurl its digital banners.

Craft visually arresting ad campaigns that resonate with your audience's aspirations. Each click, a step in the dance of conversion, brings your brand closer to the crescendo of success. Allocate your budget wisely, conducting experiments and refining your strategy based on the nuanced reactions of your digital audience.

Analytics Alchemy: The Art of Interpretation

In the grand tapestry of digital success, analytics emerge as the alchemical scrolls that decode the language of your audience's interactions. Platforms like Google Analytics, social media insights, and email metrics offer glimpses into the spells cast by your digital presence. Embrace the art of interpretation, discerning patterns and insights that guide the evolution of your online narrative.

From user behavior on your website to the resonance of your social media posts, let analytics be the compass that steers your digital ship. Understand the alchemy of data interpretation, transforming raw metrics into strategic spells that elevate your online performance.

As we conclude this extended exploration of digital marketing enchantment, remember that your online success is a perpetual symphony. Each movement—whether in content creation, social media engagement, video storytelling, influencer collaborations, email marketing, paid advertising, or analytics interpretation—is a note contributing to the harmonious crescendo of your brand's narrative.

As the conductor of this symphony, you hold the baton to shape the melodies that resonate with your audience. The enchantment is ongoing, and your journey in the digital realm is a perpetual dance of innovation and connection. May your brand's symphony echo through the digital corridors, leaving an indelible imprint on the hearts and minds of your audience.

7

Marketing Your Online Business

Congratulations, lovely entrepreneur, on recognizing the pivotal role of traffic generation in the success of your online business. Now, let's delve into the enchanting world of strategies to acquire that essential targeted traffic for your new venture. This chapter will be our magical journey through a variety of both free and paid traffic methods, offering you a comprehensive approach to gracefully market your online business.

Free Traffic Methods

1. **Content Marketing:** Embrace the art of storytelling through content creation. Regularly updating your website with beautifully crafted written content is not just beneficial for your visitors but also adds a touch of elegance to your online presence. If writing isn't your cup of tea, consider the charm of outsourcing to a skilled freelance writer. Establish a captivating presence on platforms like Medium.com, and let the soft whispers of your content resonate on social media, especially Facebook, engaging your audience and expanding your reach.

2. **Video Marketing:** Illuminate your brand with the magic of videos. Don't underestimate the enchanting impact of video content on platforms like YouTube. Create informative and delightful videos, building trust by letting the warmth of your personality shine through. Optimize your videos for search engines, focusing on the magical keywords within your niche.

3. **Podcasts:** Let your voice become a melody in the hearts of your audience through

podcasts. Discuss magical issues within your niche, conduct enchanting interviews with experts, and distribute your magical content on popular podcasting platforms. Additionally, sprinkle some fairy dust by sharing your podcasts on YouTube to maximize visibility.

4.   **Search Engine Optimization (SEO):** While requiring a bit of patience, investing in the art of SEO can create a masterpiece in the long run. Conduct thorough keyword research, optimize your website for selected keywords, and focus on weaving high-quality backlinks to enhance your external optimization.

5.   **Social Media:** Dance in the vast ballroom of social media platforms relevant to your target audience. Whether it's the elegance of Facebook, the sophistication of LinkedIn, or other platforms, concentrate on building a dedicated following by consistently providing magical content.

6.   **Email Marketing:** Though not entirely free due to the cost of the magical autoresponder service, email marketing is a highly effective spell. Build and nurture an email list

by offering enticing incentives, and design a sequence of captivating emails to maintain a magical connection with your audience over time.

7. **Guest Blogging:** Embark on a quest to contribute insightful guest posts to high-traffic blogs within your enchanted niche. This not only helps in attracting traffic but also adds a touch of magic to your website's SEO through quality backlinks.

Paid Traffic Methods

1. **Pay Per Click (PPC):** Dive into the realm of search marketing with platforms like Google and Microsoft. PPC provides a quick way to test different pages on your magical website and gather valuable insights into user behavior.

2. **Social Media Ads:** Amplify your social media presence through enchanted ads on platforms like Facebook and Instagram. Define your audience based on magical demographics, interests, and online behavior to

enhance the effectiveness of your spellbinding ad campaigns.

3.   **YouTube Ads:** Leverage YouTube's enchanted viewer base by incorporating bewitching ads within popular videos. Crafting captivating video content is key to capturing your audience's attention and guiding them through the mystical journey of your brand.

4.   **Native Ads:** Blend seamlessly into the magical world of websites by using native ads, especially effective in enchanting niches such as weight loss, make money online, and personal development. Native ads often appear more organic, increasing engagement and sharing on magical social media platforms.

As you explore these methods, remember to dance with the rhythm of your magical intuition and monitor your spending. Maintaining control over your ad spend ensures a graceful marketing strategy aligned with your budget.

Marketing Plan

To infuse a touch of magic into your marketing efforts, consider developing a comprehensive plan that seamlessly integrates both free and paid traffic methods. Carefully allocate your budget for paid advertising while gracefully managing the time constraints associated with free traffic methods. In the upcoming chapter, we'll provide a detailed 30-day plan crafted specifically for your enchanting journey toward building a 6-figure online business. Stay tuned for magical insights and strategies to gracefully propel your success!

8

∽

Your 30-Day Plan

Welcome, enchanting entrepreneur, to the transformative journey of crafting the pivotal first 30 days for your online business. As we embark on this magical odyssey, remember that meticulous planning is the key to unleashing the full potential of your digital realm. These initial days are not just a blueprint; they are a spellbook that will guide you through the enchanting months ahead. Let's delve into a comprehensive exploration of each magical step for the inaugural month of your illustrious 6-figure online business:

1. **Choose Your Niche with Passion** On the first day of your mystical journey, immerse yourself in the profound process of choosing a niche. Allow your passions to guide you as you explore subjects that not only ignite your enthusiasm but also promise financial prosperity. It's essential to strike a balance between personal interest and market demand, ensuring your chosen niche resonates with both your heart and the audience.

2. **Embark on the Art of Keyword Alchemy** Day two invites you to embark on the captivating journey of keyword research—a true art of digital alchemy. Dive into the magical realms of the free Google Keyword Planner or enlist the expertise of external alchemists to uncover the hidden gems within your niche. These enchanting keywords will be the elixirs that optimize your website and alchemize your promotional efforts into golden success.

3. **Crafting Your Goal and WHY Incantation** On the second day, step into the sacred space of crafting the vision for your online business. Set a crystal-clear goal—a beacon

guiding your path through the mystical waters of entrepreneurship. Accompany this with a WHY incantation, a powerful statement woven with the threads of your deepest motivations. Let these declarations be the spells that propel you forward, even in the face of challenges.

4. **Choose a Domain Name – The Essence of Your Digital Aura** As day three unfolds, select a domain name that encapsulates the essence of your digital aura. Whether it's directly related to your subject or a brandable concoction of magic, choose an extension (.com, .net, or .org) that aligns with your global aspirations. Your domain name is not just an address; it's the magical sigil that represents your online presence.

5. **Selecting a Web Host – The Sorcerer's Sanctuary** Dive into the enchanting world of web hosting on day three. Seek out a web host offering not just a deal but a sanctuary for your digital sorcery. Choose shared hosting wisely, considering the magical elements they provide. Connect your chosen domain name to this mystical sanctuary—a process

that, though magical, is easily guided by the numerous tutorials available.

6.   **Installing WordPress – The Spellbook of Your Digital Kingdom** On day three or four, depending on your magical schedule, immerse yourself in the installation of the WordPress platform—a spellbook that will serve as the foundation for your digital kingdom. Utilize the one-click feature provided by your web host to seamlessly integrate the magic of WordPress into your domain name.

7.   **Customize Your WordPress Haven – Crafting the Ambiance of Enchantment** Add a personal touch to your online haven on day three or four. Select a theme that not only aligns with your enchanting taste but also resonates with your target audience. Enhance your website with essential plugins, each acting as a magical ingredient in the potion of user experience. Delve into the art of adding captivating content through videos and images, transforming your digital realm into a visual feast.

8.   **Adding the Essential Pages – The Gateway to Your Magical Realm** By day five,

unveil the essential pages that will serve as the gateway to your magical realm:

a. **Home Page:** Craft an enticing first impression, a digital threshold that beckons visitors into your enchanted world.

b. **About Us Page:** Unveil the magic behind your venture, narrating the story of its inception and what you stand for.

c. **Contact Us Page:** Provide a means for your visitors to connect with you, ensuring the lines of communication are open and inviting.

d. **Terms and Conditions Page:** Establish clarity and transparency using readily available plugins, creating a harmonious digital contract.

e. **Privacy Page:** Safeguard the enchanting experience with a privacy policy, ensuring your visitors feel secure within your magical realm.

9. **Adding Niche-Related Posts – Weaving the Tapestry of Knowledge** From day

six onward, commence the art of weaving the tapestry of niche-related content onto your website canvas. Whether through the written word, magical videos, or enchanting images, let your unique voice resonate. If time is a constraint, consider outsourcing the crafting of spells (writing) while ensuring a consistent addition of magical content at least once a week.

10. **Craft Your Marketing Spellbook – Unleashing the Forces of Promotion** As the seventh day arrives, focus your magical energies on promoting your online business. Craft a spellbook of marketing strategies that align with your brand's essence. Embrace the mystical realm of tracking, adding magical elements to all your promotional efforts. Witness the magic unfold and let the insights guide your future enchantments.

In the upcoming chapter, we will embark on an in-depth exploration of scaling your online business. Prepare to unlock the secrets of expansion and witness the transformation of your digital empire into a realm of boundless possibilities. Stay tuned for more magical insights and strategies, as your journey unfolds into the realms of the extraordinary!

9

～

Elevating Your Online Business with Grace and Grandeur

As we embark on this enchanting journey through the labyrinth of online realms, the pursuit of scaling your digital dominion unveils itself like a mesmerizing tapestry. Every sorceress, whether dancing solo under the moonlight or surrounded by a coven of collaborators, reaches a pivotal moment where the allure of expanding one's influence and conjuring greater prosperity beckons. Let us delve deeper into the arcane art of scaling, where the delicate dance between strategy and collaboration takes center stage.

1. Outsource with Elegance: As the symphony of revenue becomes a harmonious melody in your digital sanctuary, consider gracefully outsourcing specific tasks. Direct your magical energies toward the realms of marketing, while entrusting skilled artisans with tasks such as weaving written enchantments, crafting mesmerizing video spells, nurturing the verdant garden of website posts, and sharing magical moments across the diverse landscapes of social media. A sorceress knows the power of delegation, building a team that complements her strengths and fuels the expansion of her magical influence.

2. Analyze and Bloom: Unveil the mystical insights concealed within the tapestry of your online domain. Install the enchanted oracle, Google Analytics, to discern the origins of your digital visitors. Peer into the magical mirror of social media analytics to identify the most bewitching posts. When navigating the realms of paid advertising, unravel the secrets of ads that cast the most potent spells. This transcendent wisdom lies in using these enchanting analytics to amplify what works and diminish the influence of what doesn't. Just as a sorceress hones her craft through years of practice, measuring the efficacy of your promotional enchantments is the key to scaling your online empire successfully.

3. Blossom in Content Magic: Unleash the power of your virtual team to cultivate an abundance of content magic. Let the enchanting winds of creativity sweep through, infusing new life into your website with captivating content. Paint the social media canvases with more of your mesmerizing posts. Illuminate the digital skies with an array of captivating videos on your YouTube channel. Allow the analytics to guide you, revealing the types of content that resonate most with your audience. The art of content creation becomes a continual dance, a celebration of creativity that captivates and inspires.

4. Elevate Your Advertising Spells: Once the stars align and reveal the efficacy of your paid advertising constellations, ascend to greater heights. Increase your investment in the celestial channels that yield the most magical results. Trim the branches of those that do not bear fruit. Be prepared to invest a portion of your enchanting profits into the advertising spells that truly work wonders. The sorceress, wise in her choices, allocates resources where they bring forth the most potent manifestations.

As we waltz through this enchanted chapter, the grand crescendo beckons. Join me as we unravel the ancient scrolls containing the secrets to a 6-figure online business. These sacred teachings, passed down through the digital ethers, will guide you on your path to prosperity, ensuring your digital realm becomes a beacon of success in the vast cosmos of online entrepreneurship. Stay enchanted, dear sorceresses, as we unveil the ultimate wisdom in the chapters yet to unfold.

10

~

Illuminating Pathways to Radiance - Best Practices for Your Majestic 6-Figure Online Empire

Embark on a transcendent journey as we traverse the radiant landscapes of online entrepreneurship, delving deeper into the sacred practices that will illuminate the path to your resplendent 6-figure online business. Let the tapestry of wisdom unfold with grace and abundance, each thread a testament to the enchanting artistry of your digital odyssey.

1. Embrace the Essence of Online Advantages:

Immerse yourself in the ethereal advantages bestowed upon those who tread the luminous avenues of online realms. Revel in the minimal entry costs, dance with the freedom to mold your empire from the heart of any locale, and savor the symphony of flexibility that allows you to shape your destiny with the fluidity of a celestial dance. Let these advantages be the North Star guiding your vessel through the uncharted waters of success.

2. Choose Your Business Model with Grace: Channel the discerning wisdom of a goddess as you survey the vast landscape of online business models. Let your selection harmonize with the melody of your financial capacity, innate skills, and the rhythmic dance of time in your life. The wrong choice can cast shadows on your journey, so choose with the elegance of a choreographed ballet, where every step resonates with the essence of your being.

3. Weave the Elegance of Proper Setup: Craft the foundational tapestry of your online sanctuary with meticulous care, eschewing the ephemeral allure of free services. Grace your venture with a registered domain, securing a realm where your digital essence can flourish. Choose impeccable web hosting as the sacred ground on which your empire will stand. Let the WordPress platform be your magical wand, turning the creation of captivating content into an enchanting endeavor that captivates the senses.

4. Set Goals and Conjure a WHY Statement: In the sacred groves of your business aspirations, set forth at least one goal and weave a WHY statement that resonates with the very core of your being. Let these be the incantations that stir the embers of determination within you, propelling you forward with unwavering resolve. Like a magical melody echoing through the corridors of your ambitions, let these aspirations be the guiding star on your celestial journey.

5. Unleash the Spell of Traffic Generation: As your digital realm takes shape, channel the majority of your energy into the mystical art of traffic generation. Like a sorceress conjuring spells to beckon spirits, understand that nothing holds more sway than the ethereal flow of visitors. Without this enchanted river, your online kingdom remains a hidden gem, waiting to be discovered in the vast expanse of the digital wilderness.

6. Promote with Graceful Finesse: Let the whispers of your online business traverse the winds, reaching the ears of those who seek its magic. Engage in the art of promotion, exploring both free and paid methods with the finesse of a seasoned dancer. Allow time to unfold its enchanted dance with free methods, and wisely steward your resources in the realm of paid promotions, creating a harmonious ballet of exposure and allure.

7. Craft a 30-Day Symphony: In the initial 30 days, let the symphony of your business unfold with grace and precision. Craft a plan that encapsulates all vital tasks, placing emphasis on the enchanting ballet of promotion and traffic generation. This magical initiation period lays the foundation for a flourishing online saga, akin to the crescendo of a symphony building to a captivating climax.

8. Elevate Your Business Essence: As your online empire blossoms to a certain crescendo, ascend to greater heights with the assistance of skilled freelancers, the unsung artists of your digital masterpiece. Allow your web pages to rise like celestial bodies in the search results, drawing in seekers with magnetic allure. Reinvest your profits, letting the alchemy of increased ad spend expand the borders of your digital kingdom, creating a mesmerizing tableau of growth and abundance.

Conclusion: A Flourishing Finale of Wisdom

In the sacred journey through these pages, a cascade of wisdom has unfolded before you, like the petals of a rare blossom revealing its innermost secrets. A radiant understanding of crafting and nurturing a 6-figure online business now resides within your grasp, a treasure trove of knowledge waiting to be unearthed. Yet, the true essence lies not in the reading alone but in the sacred dance of action.

Step forth, dear entrepreneur, armed with newfound knowledge, and let the online realms witness the birth of your digital empire. May prosperity and success accompany every keystroke and click as you embark on this enchanting odyssey. May your online venture flourish, and may the digital winds carry the whispers of your success far and wide.

Blessed be your journey, and may the magic of entrepreneurship guide your steps toward the realization of 6-figure dreams and beyond, an eternal symphony echoing through the digital corridors of destiny. May your tale be an everlasting sonnet of triumph in the vast anthology of online entrepreneurship.